BRITISH MOTORCYCLES
OF THE
1940S AND '50S

Mick Walker

T0346829

SHIRE PUBLICATIONS

SHIRE PUBLICATIONS
Bloomsbury Publishing Plc

Kemp House, Chawley Park, Oxford OX2 9PH, UK
29 Earlsfort Terrace, Dublin 2, Ireland
1385 Broadway, 5th Floor, New York, NY 10018, USA
Email: shire@bloomsbury.com
www.shirebooks.co.uk

SHIRE is a trademark of Osprey Publishing Ltd

First published in Great Britain in 2010
Transferred to digital print in 2014

A catalogue record for this book is available from the
British Library.

Shire Library no. 607
Print ISBN: 978 0 74780 805 3

Designed by Tony Truscott Designs, Sussex, UK
Typeset in Perpetua and Gill Sans
Printed and bound in India by Replika Press Private Ltd.

24 25 26 27 15 14 13 12 11 10

MIX
Paper from
responsible sources
FSC® C016779

COVER IMAGE
Cover design and photography by Peter Ashley.
Front cover image: 1948 Norton Big Four and sidecar at
the Shuttleworth Collection, Old Warden, Bedfordshire.
Back cover image: BSA Bantam, collection PA.

TITLE PAGE IMAGE
American motorcyclists bought large numbers of British-
made machines during the late 1940s. Exports were to
exceed even the Government's optimistic figures and help
pull the nation out of near bankruptcy.

CONTENTS PAGE IMAGE
The 495cc BSA A7 vertical twin, which, unlike the
Sunbeam (see page 21), had pushrod-operated valves
and was sold in much larger quantities.

ACKNOWLEDGEMENTS
Illustrations are acknowledged as follows:
Brian Wright, page 18 (top); Getty Images, pages 5, 8,
9, 11, and 25 (top). All uncredited images are from the
author's collection.

THE WOODLAND TRUST
Shire Publications supports the Woodland Trust, the UK's
leading woodland conservation charity.

www.shirebooks.co.uk
To find out more about our authors and books visit our
website. Here you will find extracts, author interviews,
details of forthcoming events and the option to sign-up for
our newsletter.

CONTENTS

INTRODUCTION

DURING THE 1940s and 1950s, the British motorcycle industry mirrored the times it passed through: the first long years of war were followed by years of great austerity in the second half of the 1940s. Then, as the 1950s began, came fresh optimism, reinforced in the second half of the decade with a series of new designs and in the final year, record sales, both at home and abroad, of the British-made machines. The competition, such as it was, was either European or American; the Japanese had not yet joined the scene on the world stage.

Peace had finally come to Europe in May 1945 and by June there was a ration of two or three gallons of petrol per month for British riders. Although modest, this of course came after years of virtually no civilian motorcycling. Fuel economy was all-important – somehow many owners could easily achieve in excess of 100 miles to the imperial gallon!

Before the end of 1945 many manufacturers were back in production, although the majority of products were often clearly either pre-war models or ones that had initially been built for military purposes. But some machines were really new, for example the Douglas 350 twin from Bristol and the Sunbeam inline twin.

Rear suspension remained largely unknown. And machines either new or used were difficult to find, even though purchase tax was a high 33.3 per cent. Why? Well, for a start the British Government wanted everything exported. In fact, even though manufacturers were eventually able to supply domestic customers, the dreaded purchase tax affected both the car and motorcycle industries for many, many years (until it was eventually replaced by VAT), as its rate was varied by the Government to either stimulate or retard the economy as it thought fit.

The early post-war years were a period of continued hardship for the British nation. Rationing of many products continued for some years, meaning that almost everything was in short supply. Motorcycles played a vital role in the immediate post-war era not only as a means of getting to work, but also for an occasional weekend or longer holiday away from

Opposite:
The assembly line at the Matchless Works motorcycle factory in London, April 1947. The machines being assembled are single-cylinder G3/L and G80 models.

one's home city, town or village. As cars were beyond the reach of all but the well-off members of society as this time, it was very much a case of travelling by tram, bus, train or pedal cycle – or of course motorcycle. So for many, the motorcycle became a means not only of easing the journey, but a source of enjoyment too.

Unlike today, British motorcycles would be maintained by the home mechanic, and the 'Blue 'Un' and 'Green 'Un' (*The Motor Cycle* and *Motor Cycling*, respectively) carried many hints and tips on how to repair, restore, modify or tune machines. Another major difference was the tyres: many people could simply not afford new tyres, even if they could be found. And there were no legal requirements regarding tread depth or the like. The result was that many riders learnt how to ride on bald ones – and also how to repair inner tubes after suffering a puncture. As the 1940s turned into the 1950s, things gradually began to improve and at long last British riders were able to purchase a post-war model. However, many designs were clearly based on old technology: suspension was only just beginning to arrive, whilst the engine remained separate from the gearbox and had a vertically split crank-case. The cylinder barrel was invariably iron – however, a few manufacturers did begin to use light alloy for the cylinder head casting. Valve gear was usually

Panther stand at the international motorcycle exhibition, Copenhagen, Denmark, 6–15 April 1951.

6

either side or overhead valve, with overhead camshafts found only on exotic racing bikes.

The electrics featured a magneto and dynamo, with a switch to the alternator during the 1950s. But even the latter was not a complete swap over. Primary drive was by chain, sometimes duplex on the more powerful larger-capacity machines, whilst lubrication was normally dry sump, with a separate oil tank under the saddle. Ancillary equipment normally included Amal carburettors, Burgess silencers and Smiths instruments. In fact, virtually everything was British made, even spark plugs from the likes of Lodge, KLG and Champion.

A major change was the widespread adoption of the telescopic front forks. These had been pioneered by the German BMW firm during the mid-1930s. And Matchless had been the first to use them in Britain, on the military G3/L 350cc single in 1941. Meanwhile, swinging-arm rear suspension was much slower to catch on, with either rigid or plunger frames still widely in use at the beginning of the 1950s.

Gearboxes, at least on larger, more expensive models, were four-speed and with foot-change. However, many ex-military models employed the old-fashioned hand-change method.

European touring on a mighty 998cc Vincent Rapide V-twin from the early 1950s.

Fred Lacey on his 1913 350cc Douglas (left), and the son of designer/engineer Erling Poppe on the latest 1949 Transverse Twin 348cc Douglas Mark 3 Sports Model, at a motorcycle rally at Newlands Corner, Surrey.

By the beginning of the 1950s a number of restrictions were lifted, making more machines (both new and used) and better-quality fuel available. During the latter half of the 1940s riders had had to make do with lower octane 'pool' petrol. The Suez Crisis of 1956 was to cause, once more, petrol rationing, although thankfully this did not last more than a few months.

As for colour, first it was military khaki drab, then overall black. But as the scars of war began to disappear so colours began to brighten; for example, the BSA A10 Golden Flash was an eye-catching metallic gold, the Triumph Thunderbird polychromatic blue, and many other shades were to appear thereafter.

Next came increases in engine size. Initially this requirement came from the export markets, notably North America. With vast mileages and straight highways the Americans needed more power, and the easiest way to achieve this was to increase engine capacity. In the immediate post-war era it was rare to find a British motorcycle of more than 500cc, but by the early 1950s, 650cc and larger became popular. Of course there were exceptions in this, for example the Vincent V-twin and the Ariel Square Four, both of which had one-litre power plants, even in the late 1940s.

As the 1950s wore on, not only did more new designs appear, but foreign competition became something of an issue. However, most continental European motorcycles of the era were in the smaller engine size bracket, usually with a maximum of 250cc. Italian and German models were the most numerous of these. For big bikes, during the period covered by this book, British bikes dominated the scene, both at home and abroad.

In the export market the Commonwealth Trade Tariff certainly helped British manufacturers, as non-British motorcycle manufacturers' products had an additional tax when sold in Commonwealth countries (such as Australia, New Zealand, Canada and the like).

Although British manufacturers did build scooters, mopeds and micro-cars, this was, in the main, left to foreign manufacturers. For their part the British two-wheeler remained largely what can be regarded as mainstream motorcycle design, consisting of traditional single- and twin-cylinder machines. And it was this type of motorcycle which the factories manufactured in ever-increasing numbers until 1959, after which production numbers and sales began to fall away. In fact 1959 was to prove a high watermark for the British motorcycle industry – a position it was never to achieve again, in terms of home sales.

1948: Film star Susan Shaw zips between buses on the new Corgi Scooter, with 98cc two-stroke engine.

WAR BIRDS

L ITERALLY HUNDREDS of thousands of motorcycles were used around the world by the military forces during the Second World War, by most nations and in most theatres.

During the Great War of 1914–18 the British with their Douglas 350s, Triumph 550s, Rudge Multis and P&Ms led the way, and so it was second time around, with Britain using more motorcycles than any other country in this latter conflict. It should be noted that for the first half of the twentieth century Britain was the leading motorcycle producer, so perhaps this state of affairs was only to be expected.

When Germany marched into Poland on 1 September 1939, many countries in Europe had been on almost a war footing since the Munich Crisis a year earlier. Britain was no different; for example, the famous Norton concern had forgone its usual challenge in the Grand Prix during the 1939 season, concentrating instead on military contracts, thanks to the persistence of its managing director, Gilbert Smith.

The machine Norton built for military service was the 490cc side-valve Model 16H single. This was essentially a 1937 civilian model with the military conversion consisting of little more than a crank-case shield pillion seat or rear carrier rack, a pair of canvas pannier bags, provision for masked lighting and a coat of khaki paint. The factory at Bracebridge Street in Birmingham also built the very similar Big Four model with larger 634cc engine size for sidecar duties. Some 100,000 16Hs were manufactured for wartime service, showing how Smith's foresight was to pay dividends. In fact, at this time, and in earlier years too, the success of the British motorcycle had been due not only to its designs and production facilities, but also to its senior management – sadly a position that was to deteriorate from the mid-1950s onwards.

Many military motorcycles, certainly those employed in the early years of the conflict, were little more than tarted-up civilian models. Modern warfare, however, as in other areas, was to display a need for more specialised machinery, the powered two-wheeler being no exception.

Opposite: RAF despatch riders, drawn from volunteers among ground staff, set out on a road and cross-country run in November 1941. The motorcycles are a mixture, including Norton 16H and BSA M20 side-valve machines.

Thanks to Norton's managing director, Gilbert Smith, the famous Birmingham factory was at the forefront of supplying motorcycles to the British Army, such as the 500cc 16H side-valve single seen here.

Like many other manufacturers Royal Enfield converted its machines for military duties.

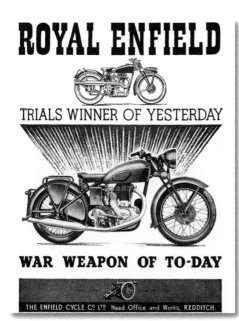

ROYAL ENFIELD

TRIALS WINNER OF YESTERDAY

WAR WEAPON OF TO-DAY

THE ENFIELD CYCLE Cº LTD Head Office and Works, REDDITCH.

In addition each country had its particular needs: the British concentrated on mainly simple single-cylinder models, the Germans complex horizontal twins (BMW and Zündapp), whilst the Americans opted for heavyweight V-twins (Harley-Davidson and Indian). But even in these countries there were many other interesting developments.

In Britain the staple diet of the military bike hardware during the war was an overhead-valve or side-valve single, usually of 350 or 500cc displacement. However, there were several types which didn't follow this line. Douglas built a prototype flat twin, James and Royal Enfield small-capacity two-strokes, Triumph various OHV twins, whilst AMC (Associated Motor Cycles) constructed an interesting prototype, using a 990cc V-twin engine.

The motorcycle was in many ways the unsung hero of the Second World War. It was to carry out a truly amazing array of tasks, but it was most widely used by the famous Despatch Riders. Although radio communications had taken over from the miles of telephone wire near the front line, which had been such a characteristic of the previous war, the bike was still important when everything else failed.

In our small corner of the Empire, we are proud that during the days of peace our product continually remained in the "front line" for unbeatable value and workmanship. It is only natural, therefore, that, to-day when the Country's needs are paramount, we again find ourselves in the "front line," going "all out" in response to the national call to defend our most valued possessions—the shores and shires of Britain and the memories of carefree runs on the dependable ARIEL.

Wartime advertisement from the dark days of October 1940: 'In our small corner of the Empire – Ariel'. This was in response to the thousands of motorcycles being built at the Selly Oak works, Birmingham, for military services.

Motorcycles were also commonly used to marshal convoys of vehicles because motorcyclists could direct traffic at one point and then leapfrog ahead, driving along the side of the road, to the next situation.

Another area in which they came into their own was scouting ahead of advancing troop columns. Some, particularly those coupled with a sidecar, carried weapons, usually either a heavy-calibre machine gun or even an anti-tank weapon.

Yet another important reason why motorcycles were so popular with the military authorities, in addition to the freedom they allowed their riders, was their cheaper cost compared with four wheels. In addition, motorcycles were also widely used by other sectors of the armed forces besides the fighting man, such as military police, and air force personnel.

Sidecars also played a vital role in a wide range of military tasks: in British service these were usually hitched to BSA M20s or Norton 16H and Big Four machines.

This 1944 advertisement says it all: 'Triumph sends another week's contribution to the end of the war and the happy days that lie ahead!'

13

Top left: Another small-capacity machine widely used in various airborne operations was the 125cc Royal Enfield Model RE.

Top right: The famous James ML (Military Lightweight) powered by a 122cc Villiers two-stroke engine.

The Norton was unusual in that it was often fitted with sidecar wheel drive, which resulted in excellent cross-country capability, combined with truly appalling handling when on the tarmac. However, the sidecar outfits of Britain and the other Allied forces were never really developed into comprehensive military vehicles, unlike those of the Axis powers, and Germany in particular.

With the advent of paratroopers it was perhaps inevitable that someone should come up with the idea of dropping a motorcycle that could be quickly assembled in the field.

Although there were others built in Italy, Germany and America, it was the British who really made a success of the concept, with specialised machines from James, Royal Enfield and Welbike. The two former designs were both fairly conventional 125cc-class two-strokes, but the Welbike was unconventional to say the least.

Enfield's effort was nicknamed the 'Flying Flea' and was powered by an engine of their own design, whereas the James effort used a Villiers motor and was known as the ML (Military Lightweight).

The third, most interesting design, the Welbike, was the idea of Lieutenant Colonel J. R. V. Dolphin and was named after the creator's home town, Welwyn in Hertfordshire. The basic idea was that the machine must fit in a cylindrical container which could be dropped by parachute, and that the bike should be ready for instant use straight from the crate. Manufactured by Excelsior, the Welbike was equipped with a 98cc Villiers engine. This was an extremely basic unit with horizontal cylinder and single speed. To fit into the narrow container small 12.5-in tyres were used. When assembled but without fuel the weight was 70 lb. Other features of Lieutenant Colonel Dolphin's design included a

Matchless G/3L power unit, showing not only the overhead-valve motor with its timing case, magneto and carburettor, but also four-speed Burman foot-change gearbox and dry sump oil tank.

collapsible steering column and handlebars and twin pannier fuel tanks astride the frame.

In terms of output, Britain built more military bikes during the war than anyone else – a staggering 440,000 of them in fact. And although Norton and BSA built the biggest number, in the author's opinion at least, the best of the bunch was the Matchless G3/L.

Despite the prototype having been evaluated and tested during 1940, the first production G3/Ls were not available until the latter half of 1941 – and it wasn't until mid-1942 that the type was in widespread service.

The Matchless G/3L 350cc OHV single with Teledraulic (telescopic) front forks was the most modern British machine to see widespread use during the Second World War.

Powered by an air-cooled OHV single with vertical cylinder, the 348cc engine put out a claimed 16bhp and had a top speed of 71 mph, but what really set the G3/L apart was its four-speed foot-change gearbox (both the BSA and Norton models were not only side-valves but had hand-change gearboxes). At 334 lb it was much lighter than the BSA and Norton. The Matchless was also the first mass-produced British motorcycle to employ a telescopic front fork assembly, instead of the long-in-the-tooth and much more cumbersome girder type. A total of 55,030 G3/Ls were delivered to the War Department.

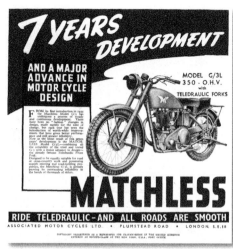

THE TWIN WITH A TEN YEAR START!

PARCEL GRID

AIR CLEANER

SPRING WHEEL

TRIUMPH *for 1949*

The modifications that have been introduced for 1949, several
of outstanding interest, have made an instant appeal to
practical hard-riding motorcyclists Basically though, the famous
Triumph range remains as before, the first and finest modern
high-performance twins in the world Prices too, remain as
before, additional costs being absorbed by improved production

THE NEW TRIUMPH INSTRUMENT NACELLE
(PATENT APPLIED FOR)

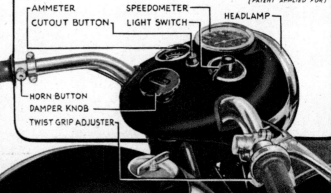

AMMETER · SPEEDOMETER · HEADLAMP
CUTOUT BUTTON · LIGHT SWITCH
HORN BUTTON
DAMPER KNOB
TWIST GRIP ADJUSTER

TRIUMPH ENGINEERING C° L™ Meriden Works, Allesley, COVENTRY

EXPORT OR DIE

BRITAIN might have been on the winning side, but when the war finally ended in the spring of 1945, the nation was at a low financial ebb. The long years of conflict had taken their toll and peace brought with it almost as many problems as had the fighting.

For the British motorcycle manufacturers, the questions were what should be produced and which markets should be pursued. At home, both the general public and the vast numbers of young former servicemen with accumulated pay provided what seemed a ready-made opportunity, with the major requirement being ride-to-work machinery.

As for imports, the British economy was in no shape to afford luxury goods from abroad. But in any case the industries of most European competitors had either been bombed off the map or systematically stripped (as in the case of BMW) of materials, machine tools and plant fittings, which were taken as war reparations by the victorious Allies.

Although the domestic market appeared to fulfil all sales requirements, wider economic forces were at play. The stark underlying fact was that Britain was as good as bankrupt. A combination of overproduction needed to win the war and borrowing from other countries, notably the USA, had left Britain with a massive trade deficit. It was a case of – as the famous phrase from Sir Stafford Cripp's budget speech bluntly put it – 'export or bust'. And as a sign of just how bad things really were, it was not until 2006 that the last payment was made to the Americans!

In motorcycle industry terms Sir Stafford Cripps specifically demanded no less than a staggering 258 per cent of the 1938 export figure by 1948. The manufacturers responded, following the series of measures outlined below, and achieved a remarkable 278 per cent by November 1947.

So just how was this miracle achieved? For a start virtually every new motorcycle built went overseas. Models were streamlined so as to make best use of men, materials and production, with Triumph, for example, building only twin-cylinder models during the immediate post-war era. But this export drive was not without its problems. And, as will be explained later,

Opposite:
In November 1948 Triumph was able to advertise 'The Twin with a Ten Year Start!' for their trend-setting five-hundred Speed Twin model.

the home market had to be satisfied by a combination of pre-war worn-out models and the sale of former WD (War Department) machinery.

Export sales meant shipping and the resultant need for extra packing materials and longer transport times than if the motorcycles had been destined for the home market. When new models or modified existing designs were first released to export markets, it meant any problems were experienced by customers thousands of miles away and were therefore much more difficult to sort out

Above: A 500cc side-valve twin-cylinder TRW RAF motorcycle. This employed an unsprung 3T frame and is pictured at RAF St Mawgan, Cornwall, in 1955.

Left: During the period immediately after the war, British riders had to make do with either ex-War Department machines (like this Matchless G3/L) or pre-war civilian models.

A 1947 348cc
Velocette KSS with
overhead camshaft
engine. A classic
British sports
bike of its era.

effectively; to say nothing of the likely damage to the reputation of both the manufacturer and Britain itself.

Aside from the use of metric instruments where necessary, there was also a need for translation of technical sales literature into a number of foreign languages, which created yet more additional work.

Quality control was another problem, not only because all British motorcycles of the era employed a number of ancillary components from outside suppliers – examples being Smiths instruments, Lucas electrical equipment and Amal carburettors – but also because of the major motorcycle manufacturers' own ruthless quest for ever more ways of keeping unit cost down. All this was at odds with building a top quality product.

But even with all these problems the British motorcycle industry did a lot of things correctly and was a vital part in putting the nation's economy back on a sounder footing. The main overseas markets during the late 1940s and early 1950s were the USA, Canada, Australia and

A 1949 Matchless
G3/L in civilian
guise, little
changed except
for its new colour
scheme.

A typical immediate post-war advertisement for ex-WD motorcycles; this one is from the London dealers, Marble Arch Motor Supplies.

Europe, in that order. In fact, it would be true to say that BSA, Norton and Triumph were soon to become household names overseas – Triumph in particular carved itself a reputation in North America to rival even the home-produced Harley-Davidson and Indian machines in the eyes of most stateside riders.

As is evident from the previous chapter, the British industry had produced more motorcycles for military use during the Second World War than any other nation, almost half a million. These comprised 126,000 BSA (mostly side-valve M20 singles), 100,000 Norton (side-valve 16H models), 80,000 AMC (mostly Matchless G3/L), 47,600 Ariel and 29,000 Royal Enfield (mainly RE two-stroke), plus several other marques in smaller quantities.

Left and below:
The Sunbeam S7
was one of the
very first new
designs to emerge
after the end of
the conflict. Its
features included
an inline overhead
camshaft (OHV)
twin-cylinder
engine, shaft final
drive and massive
balloon tyres.

During the war years the famous Donington Park (including its racing circuit) had, like several other venues scattered through England, been a home for the military authorities. Post-war Donington became a vast holding site for various war surplus vehicles, including many, many motorcycles. And it was here that several auctions were held during the immediate aftermath of the conflict. This led to vast numbers of both new and used War Department motorcycles being sold off for civilian use. And even as late as the early 1950s many of these were still being advertised by companies such as London-based Marble Arch Motor Supplies.

SUNBEAM

The Luxury Motorcycle

But eventually production of civilian models from British factories did start to reach the domestic market. The first wave of new British designs, which included the Douglas T35 three-fifty horizontal twin and the Sunbeam S8 (an inline overhead camshaft twin displacing 500cc), arrived in 1946. Another all-new design was the Swallow Gadabout – best described as an elementary scooter, powered by a 122cc Villiers two-stroke engine.

Soon the larger manufacturers such as BSA, Norton, Ariel and Royal Enfield were to bring out new 500cc parallel twin-cylinder models. This was in response to the highly successful Triumph Speed Twin, which had debuted back in 1938. In fact in their post-war advertising Triumph were to describe their new product as 'The Twin with the 10 Year Start!'

By 1949 British customers were at last being offered the chance to purchase a new machine. This Whitbys advertisement shows Swallow, James, Royal Enfield and BSA models.

Towards the end of the 1940s several other designs began to appear; these included the BSA Bantam, Royal Enfield Bullet and Velocette LE. All three were significant introductions and interesting in different ways.

The Bantam debuted in June 1948 and was to become one of the most popular BSA models of all time. However, this simple 125cc two-stroke used as its power unit an engine that was a direct copy of the pre-war German DKW RT125. The engine was a built-in unit with its three-speed gearbox and featured a vertically split crank-case. In this ran the pressed-up crank-shaft with roller big-end, a steel connecting-rod and a domed piston. The cylinder barrel was cast in iron and the head in aluminium, with the spark plug laid back at an angle. Ignition was by a flywheel-mounted magneto. An interesting feature was that the gear pedal and kickstart were on concentric shafts and enabled the machine to be kicked over whilst in gear, an extremely rare feature in Britain at that time. The engine assembly was mounted into a rigid loop frame with lightweight telescopic front forks. Certainly, the Bantam was very much the right bike at the right price, resulting in large quantities selling worldwide. In fact it remained on the BSA list until the factory finally closed during the 1970s, although by then the engine size had been increased to 175cc.

The Royal Enfield Bullet was to prove an even longer-lived design – in fact it is still being built in India at the beginning of the twenty-first century. Actually the Redditch-based Enfield concern had first used the name back in 1933. But during 1948 the post-war prototype had seen action in various motorcycle trials and was notable for its use of twin shock swinging-arm rear suspension, then unheard of in such events. When launched for the 1949 season it was made available in three guises – for use on the road, in trials or scrambles, but the essentials of the machine were the same. Its displacement

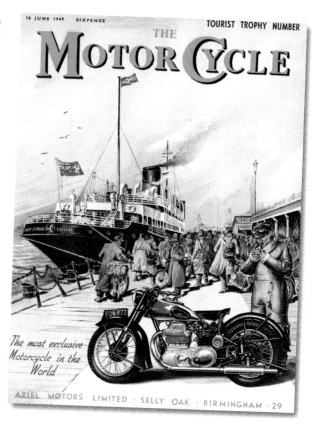

The front cover of the 16 June 1949 issue of *The Motor Cycle* with a nostalgic Ariel advertisement showing riders boarding the *Lady of Mann* steamship at Liverpool. The machine in the foreground is the 997cc Square Four.

Thinking about your first NEW motorcycle?

The B.S.A. model 350 - OHV

BSA 350

MAKE IT A BSA

THE MOST POPULAR MOTOR CYCLE IN THE WORLD

BSA (Birmingham Small Arms) was then the largest motorcycle manufacturer in the world. One of their most popular models was the 348cc B31; a 1950 model is shown.

of 346cc followed many existing Enfield features. The crank-case doubled up as the engine oil container; however, the gearbox was now bolted to the rear of the crank-case (previous Enfield overhead singles had an entirely separate gearbox).

For its time the Bullet was relatively modern – in particular its front and rear suspension, the latter courtesy of a leading-axle telescopic fork. But perhaps the most interesting, although as it turned out the least successful from a sales point of view, was the third machine, the Velocette LE (Little Engine). And when the LE made its public bow towards the end of 1948 it was most certainly different and can only be described as an innovative design.

With the LE, Velocette (previously famous for its sporting and racing machinery) discarded all preconceived ideas of what should constitute a motorcycle, and instead set about the task of translating an engine, transmission and final drive into a single 'mono' assembly regardless of the type of frame to be used and not relying upon this to hold all the bits and pieces together. The designers' aim was to produce a motorcycle for 'Mr Everyman': one that could provide continuous service over many thousands of miles without attention; a machine that answered the various criticisms which, previously, had been levelled at motorcycles; and a machine suitable for every class of road work and one that could be ridden in all weathers without special clothing being necessary. Priorities were silence, cleanliness,

The diminutive Corgi was a civilian variant of the wartime Welbike. This lightweight was powered by a 98cc Excelsior Spryt engine, weighed in at 95lb, and cost £52 plus UK purchase tax, in 1950.

RIDE A

CORGI

Economy Comfort & Speed

FEATURES—
ENGINE "SPRYT" 100 c.c.
PORTABLE - Weight 95 lbs.
ECONOMY - 125 miles per gall.
RANGE - 150 miles one filling.
COLLAPSIBLE HANDLEBARS AND SEAT.
NO GEARS. EASY PARKING.

EASILY CARRIED AND STOWED. size when Folded 53" x 20" x 13"

PRICE £52
PLUS PURCHASE TAX £14 0 10.

ORDER NOW! for early delivery. On receipt of a postcard we shall be pleased to supply the Name and Address of your nearest Stockists.

Lightweight FOLDING MOTOR CYCLE

The Civilian version of the well tried Para-troopers' "WELBIKE"

Sole distributors for Great Britain and Northern Ireland.

JACK OLDING & CO. LTD. AUDLEY HOUSE, NORTH AUDLEY STREET, W.1.
(MANUFACTURED BY BROCKHOUSE ENGINEERING (SOUTHPORT) LTD.)   Telephone: MAYFAIR 5242.

A police motorcyclist from the Leicester City Police Force stops the traffice for school children to cross safely, 1949. The machine is a Swallow Gadabout, powered by a 122cc Villiers 10D two-stroke engine, with a three-speed gearbox.

comfort, ease of starting, freedom from complicated adjustments (or the need for them), long life and economy of operation. Velocette themselves described the LE as 'Car Comfort on Two Wheels'.

Press reaction of the period is best summed up by what *The Motor Cycle* had to say in its issue of 28 October 1948, with its headline: 'Revolutionary 149cc Twin Velocette', followed by: 'Entirely New Transverse Twin Announced, with Unit Construction, Shaft-drive, Water-cooling, Rear-Springing, Telescopic Fork: A Machine Bristling with Unorthodox Features'.

So why was the LE a sales failure? (In its twenty-one years of production little more than 30,000 of them were sold and a large proportion of these to various British police forces.) There are several reasons, notably its unorthodox looks, expensive purchase price and early reliability problems. And as someone once described it, the LE was 'Britain's finest scooter' – a statement not likely to endear it to the average motorcyclist. But although it had all the weather protection of a scooter (with comprehensive enclosure and leg shields), in pure design terms it was still very much a motorcycle, albeit an unusual one.

During the period described within this chapter, life for the average British family was tough in the extreme, not helped by food rationing and – of great significance to motorcyclists – equally severe fuel rationing. So, even if you were lucky enough to own a motorcycle during the late 1940s, actually riding it was difficult, to say the least.

Petrol rationing was an unpleasant reality of post-war Britain, as featured in this 1947 Ariel advertisement.

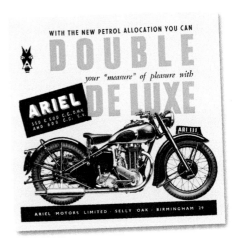

25

THE BOOM YEARS

A FTER the Second World War the real boom years for the British motorcycle industry were between 1950 and 1959. The five years of peace from 1945 were, as portrayed in the previous chapter, a period of almost unparalleled austerity for the nation, with virtually every new machine going for export to help counter the massive debt caused by the war. But as the new decade dawned things were beginning to look up. And with a better financial outlook, not only did the population have more money to spend, but at last the domestic motorcycle producers had spare capacity to meet a pent-up demand.

The early 1950s were also to see many of what are now seen as Britain's best motorcycles, including the likes of the BSA Gold Star and A10 Golden Flash, Norton Dominator, Triumph Thunderbird, Royal Enfield Meteor and Vincent Rapide. It was also a time when Britain dominated Grand Prix racing, thanks in no small part to the Norton team and its top rider, Geoff Duke.

The Norton Dominator had come via the Model 7, a five-hundred touring model with a 497cc pushrod parallel twin-cylinder engine which had debuted in November 1948, on the eve of the London Earls Court Show. However, the Featherbed-framed Dominator 88 was a much sportier model, both in performance and appearance. Whereas the Model 7 appeared typical of many other British machines of the late 1940s, with its conservative styling, single downtube frame and plunger rear suspension, the Dominator 88 used a production version of Norton's racing Roadholder front forks and the magnificent Featherbed duplex frame with up-to-the-minute swinging arm rear suspension. It is worth mentioning that the Featherbed frame was actually the creation of Belfast man Rex McCandless; initially developed for racing, it made a winning debut in the hands of Geoff Duke at Blandford in April 1950.

Soon the question on many enthusiasts' lips was, 'What about a road-going version?' Norton did put the Featherbed-framed Manx production racer on sale for 1951, but it was obvious that a roadster, at least with the Manx engine, was not practical. So even though the Birmingham company

Opposite:
1955 Norton Dominator Model 88 De Luxe with the world-renowned Featherbed duplex frame and Roadholder front forks; both developed in Grand Prix racing, with riders such as multi-World Champion Geoff Duke.

KING'S MANCHESTER SHOWROOMS WITH OVER 500 MODELS

770, CHESTER Road,
MANCHESTER
AND FOR MIDLAND RIDERS

18/20, BRISTOL Street,
BIRMINGHAM
BUT FOR GREATER BRITAIN
AND POSTAL CUSTOMERS—

KING'S·MOTORS

NEW ROAD
OXFORD

One of the largest
dealer groups in
the early-mid
1950s in Britain
was King's Motors;
their Manchester
Showrooms had a
stock of no fewer
than 500 models.

had its long running overhead-cam single
cylinder engine (from the International
model), high costs and exposed valve gear
never really made this a practical mass-
production option either.

However, as we know Norton did have
its new twin-cylinder engine, from the
Model 7. So the new Dominator was born,
a combination of the Norton racing chassis
together with the Model 7 engine and gearbox
assemblies. It was simply too good to fail and
the Dominator series was to prove the mainstay
of Norton production until the end of the
1960s.

Tested throughout the summer of 1951,
the production version made its public debut
at the beginning of November 1951, ready for
the 1952 season. At first all supplies went for
export; this was soon rectified. The only
problem Norton faced was one of cost, the

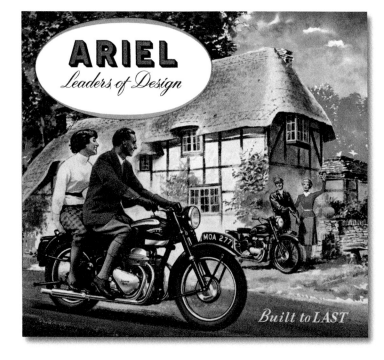

With its 'Leaders
of Design' the
Ariel marque
offered a range of
models spanning
200cc to 1000cc
during the mid-
1950s.

In contrast to
the ultra-sporting
Gold Star was the
Velocette MAC
350. This 1953
version
still has a rigid
(unsprung) frame.

Dominator 88 being some 20 per cent more expensive than a comparable BSA or Triumph. The BSA A7 Star Twin cost £222 and the Triumph Tiger 100 was £223, whereas the new Norton came in at £260 (all these figures include British purchase tax). Producing some 30bhp, the Dominator 88 could easily top 90 mph in 1952.

In late September 1949, Triumph Engineering of Meriden near Coventry had launched a 650 twin in a blaze of publicity: the first three production models having been taken to the Montlhéry circuit, just south of Paris, where they proceeded to cover 500 miles, ending the display with a flying lap

The BSA Gold Star
was the ultimate
British sporting
single of its era,
particularly in its
definitive form, the
DBD 34 Clubmans
with its powerful
499cc all-alloy
engine and RRT2
close-ratio
gearbox.

Matchless owners (a G80 five-hundred single is shown) are encouraged to go touring on the Continent in this August 1953 advertisement.

Motorcycle clubs were very popular during the 1950s. Here members of the Loughborough College Motor Club are at the BSA factory, Birmingham, on 20 February 1952.

of over 100 mph. Named the Thunderbird, the newcomer was described thus in the factory press release:

A machine designed primarily for sustained high speeds on the vast, smooth highways of America, South Africa and Australia [Britain's three principal export markets at the time], with an engine developing 34bhp at 6,000rpm and a total weight of little more than the famous 500cc Speed Twin. Truly a mount to whet the interest of every enthusiast!

As with the Speed Twin, the Thunderbird was the work of the legendary designer, Edward Turner. Factory graphs revealed that the Thunderbird engine developed the same power at 4,000rpm as the Speed Twin did at 6,000rpm. As for power output the Thunderbird produced 7bhp more than the Speed Twin at similar engine speed. But the biggest advantage was not to be found in sheer horsepower at high engine revolutions: instead, it was that the larger twin had a flat torque curve and superior low-down pulling power. This was also a reason why the Thunderbird was to prove so popular in sidecar circles.

BSA, then the largest motorcycle manufacturer in the world, had two glamour models during the first half of the 1950s, the 650 A10 Golden Flash twin and the Gold Star sporting single. And in truth the two could not have been more different, although each was a great success in its own area of the motorcycle world.

Prior to the original Gold Star (the 500 M24 had arrived in the late 1930s), BSA had been known for sound, reliable, value-for-money, but hardly

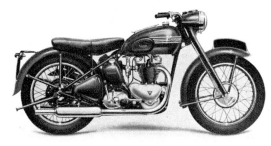

COMFORT FOR TWO — *Scientifically designed*

THE

TRIUMPH

TWIN-SEAT

The Triumph "Twin-Seat" provides an attractive alternative to the normal saddle and pillion seat. To the long distance solo man it gives a first class riding position with the option of a change of position to counter fatigue Two-up, with the passenger on the same seat as the driver, there are obvious advantages from a controllability point of view.

Length 25¼ inches.
Width in centre, 12¼ inches.
Width at rear, 9 inches.
Weight 9¼ lbs. (same weight as separate saddle and pillion seat).

1 Luxurious all-over Latex Foam cushion moulded for maximum comfort and stability.
2. Cushion covered in tough, long wearing, black "V Y N I D E" completely waterproof.
3. Internal cell forms prevent rolling or sway at any speed.
4 Steel base pan specially shaped to permit maximum depth of cushion where needed.
5. Rear edge of pan formed into lip for passenger's comfort when machine is accelerating.
6 Three point mountings at front, centre and rear.

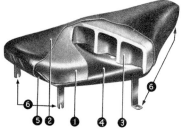

TRIUMPH ENGINEERING CO. LTD. Meriden Works, Allesley, COVENTRY

The Triumph factory made much of its twin-seat (more commonly known as the dual seat); this was soon adopted throughout the industry, replacing the original single saddle and pillion seat.

A Triumph 650
Thunderbird in a
workshop setting,
c. 1952.

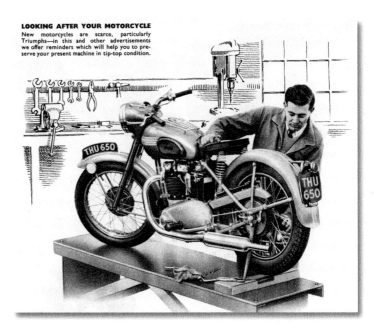

LOOKING AFTER YOUR MOTORCYCLE
New motorcycles are scarce, particularly
Triumphs—in this and other advertisements
we offer reminders which will help you to pre-
serve your present machine in tip-top condition.

sporting bikes. But the 'Goldie' changed all that, right from its successful
debut at Brooklands in June 1937, where it won a 'Gold Star' for its 100
mph-plus lap – and hence the name.

After the war came the new 348cc B32, soon followed by the 499cc B34.
Development saw plunger and finally swinging-arm frames, whilst the engine
progressed from small-fin to big-fin types by the mid-1950s. But what made
the Gold Star so successful was its ability to perform in virtually every field
– a feat never matched so convincingly by any other motorcycle. Whether it
was as a roadster (in both touring and sporting guise), clubmans or endurance
racing, scrambles (moto-cross), trials, sprinting or the ISDT (International
Six Days Trials), the legendary Gold Star performed with distinction. Not
only that, but a whole generation of post-war British youth saw the machine
as the café racer supreme, featuring such icons as the RRT2 close-ratio
gearbox, Amal GP carburettor and 190 mm front brake.

Compared to the sporting nature of the Gold Star single, the A10 Golden
Flash was almost the complete opposite, being very much a reliable
workhorse. But together with the Gold Star and Bantam, the Golden Flash
is now regarded as one of the truly classic BSA models of the marque's great
days of the 1950s. *Motor Cycling* dated 6 October 1949 (together with *The
Motor Cycle*) brought to the public's attention the arrival of a newcomer that
would earn not only worldwide sales for its manufacturers, but genuine love
and affection from its enthusiastic owners.

The BSA B31 (350) and B33 (500) heavyweight singles were popular throughout the 1950s.

Technically speaking, the 646cc Golden Flash bore a strong resemblance to the 495cc A7 (introduced in September 1946). But there were several important changes – that were in fact to lead directly to a revised 'Mark 2' version of the A7, which itself arrived in October 1950, with its engine size now 497cc.

Although advance details of the A10 six-fifty had been published in early October, it was not until the end of that month and the opening of the Earls Court Show that the new BSA twin was actually put on display to the general public. Initially, the Golden Flash was available in standard (rigid frame) and deluxe (plunger frame) guises. However, from the 1952 model year the rigid frame had been dispensed with.

The police were regular users of motorcycles. Members of the East Sussex Constabulary are seen here with their BSA A10 Golden Flash machines in 1953.

A December 1952 advertisement for the newly released Royal Enfield 700 Meteor. It was essentially an enlarged 500 Twin, with dual front brake, and much more powerful engine.

Another Royal Enfield was the Bullet single, built in both 348 and 499cc engine sizes. A modernised version is still being built in India today.

In solo form the machine would reach 96 mph and with a BSA-made single-seat sidecar the figure was reduced to 70 mph. Obviously, a Golden Flash fitted with a double adult-type chair would have less speed. *The Motor Cycle* tested just such an outfit: 'The best maximum cruising speed with the sidecar fitted appeared to be anything from 55 to 65 mph'. But perhaps even more impressive was, 'at the lower end of the scale the outfit would trickle along in top gear without snatch at speeds of just over 20 mph'. And this provides a view of just why the BSA twin was so highly rated, thanks in no small part to excellent engine torque. This, combined with its general reliability, good fuel economy and comfort, and the large BSA dealer network, helped build its reputation.

The final major change to the A10 came for the 1954 season, with a brand new swinging arm frame, together with a revised engine and gearbox

(the latter assemblies mainly altered to suit the new chassis).

An interesting rider's-eye views of the Bullet, with its headlamp nacelle containing the 120mph Smiths speedometer, amp gauge and lighting switch.

The Royal Enfield Meteor arrived at the end of 1952, in time for the 1953 season. What really made it notable, though, was that at the time it was Britain's largest model with vertical cylinders and two pots; its actual displacement was 692cc, even though Enfield simply marketed it as the 700 Meteor. Incidentally, in the USA it was sold as the Indian Trailblazer – even more confusing!

At the 1952 Earls Court Show the Meteor was displayed hitched to a Watsonian sidecar, the factory believing its new model would have a particular appeal to the sidecar user, whether he was keen on taking the family out for a sedate tour of the countryside, or for fast road work. Remember, Britain had not yet embraced the small affordable car as it did later in the decade, with the arrival of the Mini. So at the time of the Meteor's launch there was still

A magnificent setting for a magnificent motorcycle – a 1952 Vincent Comet five-hundred single with a stately home (Audley End) as its backdrop.

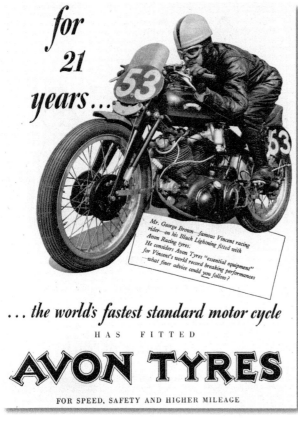
An Avon Tyres advertisement from June 1950, proclaiming Vincent as the 'world's fastest standard motorcycle'.

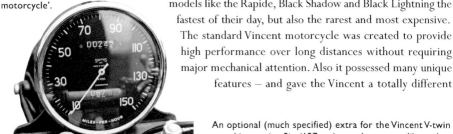

a considerable demand for a motorcycle capable of sidecar work. The show Meteor was equipped as standard with a specially robust rear fork, designed to ensure the spring-frame was entirely suitable to withstand the stresses imposed by high-speed sidecar duties. This applied equally to either a single-seat sports chair or one of the larger double adult sidecars, which were very much in vogue at the time.

In solo trim, the Meteor was, for its time, an extremely fleet sports-tourer. Heavier than the well-proven 500 Twin Enfield by a mere 10 lb, the larger engine had an impressive power-to-weight ratio. It also had plenty of flexible muscle, hence its equal appeal as a sidecar machine. But perhaps its weak point was the use of separate cylinder heads and barrels; these did not provide the rigidity of its BSA, Triumph and Norton rivals.

Of all the British motorcycles of the first half of the 1950s the Stevenage-built Vincent is the one generating the highest prices in today's classic motorcycle world. The reason is not hard to find: not only were models like the Rapide, Black Shadow and Black Lightning the fastest of their day, but also the rarest and most expensive. The standard Vincent motorcycle was created to provide high performance over long distances without requiring major mechanical attention. Also it possessed many unique features – and gave the Vincent a totally different

An optional (much specified) extra for the Vincent V-twin was this massive 5in (127mm) speedometer, calibrated to 150mph.

The 998cc
(84 x 90mm)
50-degree
overhead-valve
Vincent V-twin
engine.

Typical mid-1950s
head gear for
the British
motorcyclist.
Feridax helmets
are shown here;
others including
Corker, Everoak
and Stadium were
also popular.

style to more mainstream models. Then there was the 998cc V-turn engine, which besides being relatively unstressed was during its day tagged 'The World's Fastest Standard Motorcycle'.

In terms of performance, as a general rule of thumb, as they left the factory the Rapide (touring model) could achieve 110 mph, Black Shadow (sports model) 125 mph and Black Lightning (racing model) 140 mph.

The final versions, the D series, were built in December 1955. Approximately 11,000 Vincent HRD and Vincent models were built between 1946 and 1955. Over 6,000 of these were sold in Britain and the remainder were exported to fifty-nine countries around the world. Some 6,850 were twins; the others, 4,150 of them, were single. These latter bikes were mainly the Comet, but there were a small number of the now very rare Grey Flash racers; both singles had a capacity of 499cc.

The Glow of Youth —
"Pride of Possession"

LKV 30

BRITAIN'S LEADING LIGHTWEIGHT

Francis-Barnett

FRANCIS & BARNETT LTD., LOWER FORD ST., COVENTRY

TELEPHONE: COVENTRY 3054   TELEGRAMS: FRANBAR COVENTRY

COMMUTER BIKES –
CHEAP AND CHEERFUL

W ITH THEIR ROLE now neatly filled by a second (or even third) car, it might seem unlikely but much of Britain in the 1940s and 1950s went to work, rest and play on one of the myriad small-capacity two-stroke motorcycles manufactured by the domestic bike builders.

Actually, a large percentage of motorcycles built in Britain during the period covered by this book were not the much loved large-capacity sporting single- and two-cylinder four-strokes that are today so fondly remembered by the classic enthusiasts. Most were simple piston-port induction two-strokes from the likes of BSA, Francis-Barnett, James and Royal Enfield, to name just a few.

Many would be right to argue that the foundation of a mass-market motorcycle firm lies in the design and production of its bread-and-butter models. As Honda was to prove with its multi-million-selling Super Cub 'step-thru' design, such machines make a vital contribution towards the development of larger, more expensive machines.

The 'Super Cub' of the BSA empire was the Bantam, a model series built in relatively large quantities from the late 1940s until the early 1970s. But surprisingly, what became one of BSA's best-selling models ever didn't have its roots in Birmingham. Instead, it came about from the opportunity to make use of German technology; to be precise, the pre-war DKW RT125. This had been designed by Hermann Weber towards the end of the 1930s and entered production on the eve of war in 1939. The basis of both the DKW design and the Bantam was the engine, a single-cylinder two-stroke, which was a built-in unit with a three-speed, foot-change gearbox.

The new 123cc machine was officially announced in June 1948 as the D1, but it soon became known as the Bantam. At first, it was listed for export only. The engine was fitted to an all-welded, rigid frame – at the time, an innovation for BSA – with a single main tube running around the power unit, and rear loops to the wheel. The front forks were simple telescopics with internal springs, but no damping, and the legs slid on grease-lubricated, sintered bronze bushes fitted to the outer tubes.

Opposite:
A 1952
advertisement
for the Coventry-
based Francis-
Barnett marque,
then part of the
giant Associated
Motor Cycles
(AMC).

Typical British ride-to-work mount of the immediate post-war era, the Ambassador with 197cc Villiers 6E engine and integral three-speed foot-change gearbox. It could reach 55mph and return an economical 110 mpg. This advertisement dates from November 1948.

The 125cc BSA Bantam D1 was officially announced in June 1948 and although it went on to become one of the top-selling British motorcycles of all time, it was actually developed from a German DKW model.

From 1950 buyers could opt for a plunger suspension chassis rather than a rigid frame. In 1954 a larger-engined D3, with a capacity of 148cc, was introduced to complement the D1.

At the end of 1957, the D3 was discontinued, and for 1958, the 172cc D5 made its debut. However, this lasted for only twelve months before the

improved D7 arrived to replace it. By this time, all Bantams, except the D1, sported swinging-arm rear suspension. The D7 continued in production until 1966, with the long-running D1 finally axed in 1963. The last examples of the Bantam (the D14/4 and D175) were built in 1971.

As for Royal Enfield, its RE or 'Flying Flea' was conceived just as war was about to begin in 1939, and like the BSA Bantam, it owed much to a German DKW design (this time the RT98 model). Featuring a 125cc engine size it was subsequently built by the Redditch-based Enfield factory in both civilian and military guises as the RE and Flying Flea respectively.

A simple diamond frame was used, constructed in circular steel tubing, whereas the front fork was quite unusual, being built up from two pressed steel girders linked at the top and bottom to the steering head by a series of rubber bands – a system pioneered by DKW from the mid-1930s. In their advertising Royal Enfield was to promote the RE as 'the lightest 125cc motorcycle'. But during the immediate post-war era many ex-military Flying Fleas were put back into civilian guise and sold off to a transport-hungry British public.

As the 1940s came to a close, telescopic front forks came very much into vogue – even on ultra-lightweight machines.

During November 1950, a new RE125 was announced (known as the RE2). This came in response to falling sales from the outgoing model (even though it had been updated with telescopic forks only twelve months earlier).

At the centre of the new model was a freshly designed and much neater engine assembly. And it would be true to say that it showed much DKW RT125/BSA Bantam influence. Like these two machines the latest Royal Enfield featured a three-speed foot-change gearbox in unit with the engine. But it was in the area of chassis design that the RE2 missed the boat. Whereas it was now possible to specify plunger rear suspension as a cost option on the BSA, Enfield chose to stick with a rigid frame, probably for cost reasons. In retrospect what they should have done was to produce the RE125 with a brand new swinging-arm frame – which had already been introduced on larger

The Royal Enfield RE with 125cc single-cylinder two-stroke of the company's own design. This illustration dates from spring 1952.

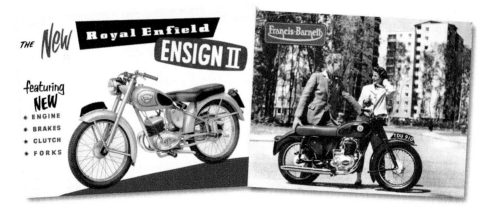

Above: The Royal Enfield Ensign, with its 148cc (56 x 60mm) was a development of the immediate post-war RE125 from the same factory. This brochure dates from 1955.

Above right: A 1959 Francis-Barnett Cruiser 80 with the ill-fated 249cc AMC engine.

models, such as the new 350 Bullet and 500 Twin. In fact, in the author's opinion the factory could have gone a stage further and given the machine four instead of three speeds. This surely would have given the little Enfield a distinctive edge in the commuter sales war of the early 1950s. Instead Royal Enfield paid the price by always running a poor second behind the top-selling BSA product.

At the end of 1952 Enfield launched the Ensign, which used a 148cc version of the RE2 engine. But the biggest change was to the frame. At first glance this appeared to have plunger rear suspension with exposed springs, but in reality this was a pivoted fork. It was crude to say the least – the springs were simply held in place as on a plunger frame!

A revised version, the Ensign II, debuted in autumn 1955, at the London Earls Court Show. There were a number of improvements, notably the

Front cover from the 1954 James brochure. The model shown is the 225cc Model K12 Colonel, at that time the largest capacity machine offered by the Birmingham concern.

engine, more robust front forks and more powerful brakes.

Finally in 1959, came the Prince; although still a 148cc two-stroke, it differed in several ways from the Ensign. The most notable difference was, at last, the introduction of a swinging-arm frame with twin hydraulically damped shock absorber units. The last Prince was built in 1962.

Both Francis-Barnett and James used bought-in Villiers engines, as did virtually every other British two-stroke motorcycle of the 1940s and 1950s, except BSA and Royal Enfield. The Villiers Engineering Company of Wolverhampton had produced its first engine back in 1912. And between 1948 and late 1956 Villiers produced no fewer than one million engines (including stationary and industrial units). It is also worth pointing out that the company also had factories in Spain and Australia, but the bulk of Villiers engines were still manufactured in Britain.

AMC (Associated Motor Cycles) had taken over Francis-Barnett of Coventry in June 1947 and James (the firm based in Greet, Birmingham)

The James brand had a good reputation for producing cheap but reliable small-capacity bikes. This 1955 photograph shows three of their models (from left to right): 200 Commando (trials), 200 Captain and 150

The Comet 100 (actually 98cc) was the cheapest model in the James line-up. Maximum speed was 40mph (although no speedometer was fitted as it was not required by law in UK motorcycles of under 100cc at the time). This is a 1958 machine.

during November 1950. Both marques were long-established builders of small-capacity motorcycles, Francis-Barnett beginning in 1919, James in 1880 (although motorcycles did not arrive until 1902).

During the period covered by this book, Francis-Barnett models included the Merlin, Falcon, Powerbike, Kestrel, Cruiser and Plover. And no, the Powerbike was not the top-of-the range speed machine, but instead an autocycle powered by a 98cc Villiers JDL unit and hard pushed to reach 30 mph! But most were initially powered by 122cc and 197cc engines, that was until Villiers introduced their 225cc 1H unit in 1954. By 1957 Francis-Barnett (and James) had started using AMC engines, including one of 249cc. However, this was not popular with buyers, as the Villiers engines were more reliable.

The post-war James models included the ML125, 98cc Comet, Superlux autocycle, Cadet, Commodore, 197cc Captain and from late 1954 the 225cc Colonel. And like Francis-Barnett, James also used AMC engines (of 149cc and 249cc capacities).

Besides BSA, Royal Enfield, Francis-Barnett and James, other British manufacturers of two-stroke-engined commuter motorcycles were: Aberdale, ABJ, AJW, Ambassador, BAC, Bond, Bown, Corgi, Cotton, DMW,

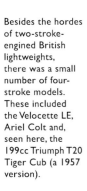

Besides lightweight motorcycles, there was also the forerunner of the moped, the autocycle. Several British manufacturers built these during the 1940s and early 1950s, including New Hudson. Like most, this was powered by a 98cc Villiers two-stroke engine.

Besides the hordes of two-stroke-engined British lightweights, there was a small number of four-stroke models. These included the Velocette LE, Ariel Colt and, seen here, the 199cc Triumph T20 Tiger Cub (a 1957 version).

DOT, Excelsior, FLM, Greeves, HJH, Mercury, New Hudson, Norman, OEC, Panther, Sun and Tandon. Some of these latter marques used Anzani, Excelsior or JAP engines. And then there were the limited number of bikes powered by four-stroke engines. Into this category came the Triumph Terrier (149cc) and Tiger Cub (199cc), Ariel Colt (200cc) and Velocette LE (150 and later 200cc).

But, in truth, British commuter bikes of the immediate post-war era were almost universally two-strokes. The reason for this was simply cost-related, it being much cheaper to manufacture a small two-stroke than the more complicated four-stroke type. Additionally, a two-stroke was much more straightforward, and therefore easier for the home mechanic to maintain. Remember, in those far-off days there was a level of austerity that can hardly be imagined at the beginning of the twenty-first century.

During the late 1940s and early 1950s life was still pretty basic. And this was reflected in people's transport, which for the working man often meant a bicycle or lightweight motorcycle. As for car ownership, this was still a distant dream for the majority of the British population.

One journalist described it as 'Britain's best scooter'. But although it offered excellent weather protection, the Velocette LE (Little Engine) was very much a motorcycle.

THE AMAZING NEW

Velocette

FEATURES

Velocette

VELOCE LTD · YORK ROAD · HALL GREEN · BIRMINGHAM

Velocette

SPRING-TIME *you had a*

The B.S.A. Golden Flash is a good-looker—and its performance and comfort are every bit as good as its appearance suggests. The 650 O.H.V. Twin engine has all the power and flexibility you could wish for, and is remarkably silent; the 4-speed gearbox is smooth and easy in operation, whilst the duplex frame design gives complete riding comfort, hairline steering and perfect road-holding. The "Bantam" is the 'go-anywhere' machine that made low-cost motor-cycling popular.

THE MOST POPULAR MOTOR CYCLE IN THE WORL

BSA WINNERS OF THE MAUDES TROPHY

SIDECARS – FAMILY TRANSPORT

During the immediate post-war period the sidecar was a familiar sight on British roads. In fact the sidecar was built by a wide range of firms in many guises – everything from a single seat sports to massive double adult models; there were even tradesman's box types, whilst the AA (Automobile Association) and RAC (Royal Automobile Club) used them as patrol vehicles. The earliest examples of the sidecar arrived just after the turn of the twentieth century and by 1903 a couple of firms were already offering them for sale. Most sidecar bodies at this time were of wickerwork to cut down on weight.

Following the First World War there was an urgent need to provide motorised transport for the family. This meant that not only were there many specialised sidecar manufacturers, but also that several early motorcycle producers entered into the field. The latter group included such names as BSA, Royal Enfield, Sunbeam, Douglas, P&M (Phelon & Moore – later known as Panther), Ariel, Triumph, Chater-Lea, Dunelt, New Imperial and Raleigh.

Besides the British sidecar industry, the other major European country to offer sidecars was Germany in the shape of BMW and Steib. BMW built their own sidecars for many years, whilst Steib built only 'chairs' and were represented in Britain by the dealers Bryants of Biggleswade in Bedfordshire until 1938, and thereafter by Frazer Nash of Middlesex.

In 1936 there were half a million motorcycles on British roads, of which no less than a quarter had a sidecar fitted, whilst by 1939 there were three sidecar combinations to every ten solos. The third wheel had proved it was here to stay.

But the sidecar's real heyday was that of the late 1940s and throughout the 1950s. With the ending of the war, established sidecar manufacturers returned with renewed energy. And with increased demand many new firms sprang up to join the established names, such as Swallow, Blacknell, Canterbury, Busmar, Surrey, Gerrard and Panther.

The sidecar was very much a part of British motorcycling and because so many machines were likely to haul a sidecar, motorcycle manufacturers built

Opposite:
For many years BSA offered its own range of sidecars. This March 1953 advertisement has 646cc A10 Golden Flash and BSA sports chair; also in the picture is a 125cc Bantam D1 commuter bike.

Before the arrival of the small, affordable car, many British families relied on the motorcycle and sidecar combination. This side-valve Norton 600cc Big Four and double adult 'chair' is pictured here during the late 1940s.

Above: The AA employed BSA M21 and box sidecar outfit for its patrol duties on British roads during the 1950s.

Right: A Swallow double adult sidecar dating from the early 1950s.

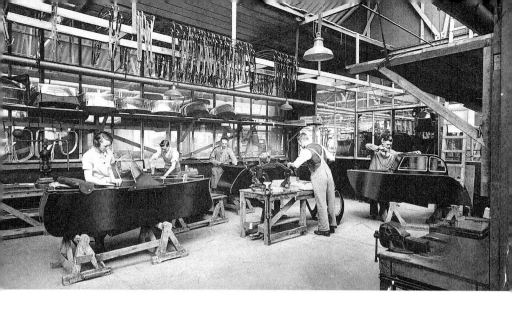

frames that could not only stand the strain of having a third wheel fitted, but also provided lugs to these frames for the express purpose of fitting a 'chair'. Indeed, most manufacturers actually designed their larger capacity machines with the sidecar in mind. Some, for example Panther, openly advertised their products as 'sidecar tugs'.

Part of the Birmingham Watsonian sidecar factory, showing assembly taking place.

1954 MODELS

THE CHAMPION'S CHOICE—

Watsonian SIDECARS

FOR TOURING—

FOR RACING—

Watsonian SIDECARS

FOR TRIALS—

Watsonian SIDECARS

WHAT QUALITY – WHAT VALUE – WATSONIAN!

Watsonian was Britain's largest sidecar manufacturer. This 1954 brochure cover shows that the Birmingham company built sidecars for every purpose including touring, racing and trials.

49

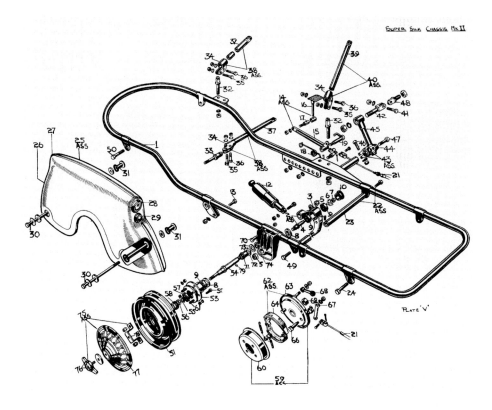

A factory drawing of the Watsonian Super Silk Mark II sidecar chassis.

Initially, as mentioned previously, the British public had to make do with either pre-war motorcycles or ex-WD bikes. Neither of these options posed a real problem for their owners who wished to fit a sidecar, simply because not only were British motorcycles of the 1930s constructed for sidecar duties, but so too were the majority of the military models.

If one particular motorcycle manufacturer epitomised the British sidecar machine, it was without doubt the Panther. With their works in Cleckheaton, West Yorkshire, the company had originally been known as P&M (Phelon & Moore). But by the 1940s P&M had given way to Panther – with a panther's head as its emblem.

A feature of the Panther machines was the use of a sloping cylinder – the 598cc Model 100 and later (from 1959) the 646cc Model 120. Both machines were single cylinders, although at first glance due to a twin-port cylinder head and thus two exhaust header pipes and two silencers (one each side of the machine) the Panther might appear to be a twin. Actually, with that massive cylinder, in both engine capacities, the outstanding feature was torque, the engine firing every lamp-post! Which helps explain just why the

The Panther 600 or 650cc single cylinder engine was probably the premier sidecar device, with its massive pulling power. The example shown here was specially prepared for the arduous International Six Days Trial (ISDT), held in 1950 in Wales.

Panther 100 or 120 made such a good sidecar tug. Even the largest 'chair' was not beyond one of the Panther sloper singles.

Although during the period of this book Panther tried other smaller capacity models – using bought-in Villiers engines or the 65 (250cc) and 75 (350cc) OHV singles, or even (in the mid-1950s) importing French Terrot scooters, and later still producing its own scooter (the Princess) – it was always their big sloper singles for which Panther were most famous.

The first post-war Model 100 was very much in the pre-war mould, with its rigid frame and girder forks. And although the girders were replaced by Dowty-made teles from 1949, it was still possible to buy a rigid-frame model until as late as 1956. The new 100S (swinging-arm) model made its debut in 1954, with the larger 120S arriving in 1959. Panther also supplied complete sidecar outfits until production finally ended in the mid-1960s. In total some

Sidecar chassis on a specially constructed jig being brazed at a low temperature.

Another excellent choice, but considerably more expensive, was the 997cc Ariel 4G Mark II Square Four, seen here in 1955.

Below left: The Panther Model 100 (and later the Model 120) were ideally suited to sidecar duties. As this 1953 advertisement says, 'Acknowledged by the public as the best all round value on the market for power, flexibility and economy with performance.'

Below right: Panther Model 120 arrived in 1959 and was the definitive version of the big single-cylinder sidecar tug. Production ceased in the mid-1960s.

12,000 of the Model 100 and 2,500 of the Model 120 were built; almost all were used for sidecar work.

There was a host of other British motorcycles available to the sidecar user. Other makes and models include BSA A7/A10, AJS and Matchless twins and singles, Triumph Thunderbird, Ariel Huntmaster 650 twin, the 1000cc

A 1958 BSA A10 Golden Flash hitched to a Watsonian Monarch single-seater sports sidecar.

A 499cc Velocette Venom and Watsonian sidecar, proving that many single cylinder British machines were also used as sidecar outfits.

Canterbury logo; the factory was based in South Ockendon, Romford, Essex.

Square Four and VB 600 side-valve single, Velocette MSS 500 single and (last, but certainly not least) the Vincent Rapide 1000cc, V-twin.

Many other machines were fitted to a sidecar – even several scooters! But, with the advent of the affordable small car at the very end of the 1950s, the day of the sidecar outfit came to an end, almost overnight in fact.

INDIAN SUMMER

TOWARDS the end of the 1950s, and with living standards in Britain on the rise, there was more money to spend. Motorcycle sales actually peaked in 1959, before the industry was to see not only increased competition from abroad (notably Japan), but also the arrival of the small car sales boom (headed by the Mini). But for the last half of the 1950s the sun shone on the British motorcycle. This period also saw a number of new models enter production, including a crop of 250cc machines; these were brought out in anticipation of impending laws limiting learner riders to this engine size – another move that was to have an adverse effect on domestic motorcycle sales. Another future problem would be the ending of the Commonwealth Tariff on non-British motorcycles. So the five years from the beginning of 1955 to the end of 1959 can in retrospect be seen as truly golden years for the industry, its dealers and its riders.

In September 1955 both Norton and AMC (AJS and Matchless) announced 600cc versions of their existing 500cc twins. The Norton was the Dominator 99, whilst the AMC machines were the AJS Model 30 and Matchless G11. As *The Motor Cycle* pointed out:

> For the solo rider in Britain, whether he requires extra speed or not, there are advantages accruing from the use of increased capacity. Improved torque means better low-speed pulling; and reduced engine wear and tear is likely to be achieved since the power unit, for most of its life, is operating comfortably within its limits.

Official figures gave the maximum speeds for the newcomers as: Norton 99, 96 mph and the AMC twins, 92 mph – in both cases some 10 mph faster than their respective 500cc brothers.

Besides being quicker the Norton also had the advantage in the road-holding stakes with its superior frame and suspension. Their BSA and Triumph rivals already had 650s. A more sporty version of the Triumph, the Tiger 110 had been introduced at the Paris Show back in October 1953. The first

Opposite:
Enclosure was a feature of British motorcycle design during the late 1950s. Typical is this 1959 Francis-Barnett Cruiser 84, with 249cc AMC engine. The entire rear of the machine was enclosed from behind the engine cylinder. The leg shields were also a standard fitment, as was the substantial front mudguard.

The BSA 500 Shooting Star vertical twin was the sports version of the popular A7 touring model. This 1958 model is typical of the breed and is finished in polychromic green, a feature of the Shooting Star. Maximum speed was approaching 100 mph.

version of a sporting BSA 650 twin had come in the same year in the shape of the Super Flash. But this model only lasted a few months before it was superseded by the Road Rocket; both were primarily aimed at the Stateside market. And it was not until June 1956 that British riders learned that the Road Rocket was to be included in BSA's 1957 programme. It was certainly worth the wait as BSA's official figures of 40bhp and 105 mph were dubbed conservative by *Motor Cycling*, whose journalist found it capable of achieving 109 mph.

When the 1958 BSA model range was announced in mid-1957, not only were there several changes to the A10 Golden Flash tourer, but a new model, the Super Rocket, replaced the Road Rocket. Performance was on a par with the outgoing Road Rocket.

In the summer of 1958 a 649cc Triumph Tiger 110 had won the prestigious Thruxton 500-mile endurance race, ridden by Mike Hailwood and Dan Shorey. However, what was not realised at the time was that this machine was in fact the prototype for Triumph's most famous model, the legendary Bonneville. Coded T120, it differed from other large-capacity British machines of the late 1950s by having twin carburettors. It was also the fastest 650 of its era, the 1959 Bonneville having a top speed of 122 mph. However, unlike BSA, Triumph did not axe the Tiger 110, which was almost a Bonneville in a slightly lower tune and with a single carburettor.

TRIUMPH TECHNICAL SUPERIORITY GIVES YOU THE BEST IN
PERFORMANCE AND DEPENDABILITY

THE value of the contribution that Triumph has made to the motorcycling world during the past fifty years is almost impossible to assess. Right from the start Triumph set a pace in design and development which has been unrivalled. When ignition systems, for instance, were very uncertain in the earliest days, Triumph were the first to standardise the magneto—an instrument whose supremacy today is threatened by the Triumph pioneered A.C. electrical system. When engine design was fluid, Triumph settled on a simple reliable single cylinder unit which became the standard for the Industry until it, in its turn, was ousted by the Triumph developed vertical twin, so extensively used at the present time.

Now, Triumph offers, in addition to a range of brilliant twins, a new conception of lightweight design and performance in the "Terrier" and "Tiger Cub" models, which yet again emphasise the technical superiority of the Triumph product.

Always, Triumph have built motorcycles which are a joy to own and a thrill to ride, and never has it been truer to say this than today.

This Catalogue Published 31st October, 1953

The Best Motorcycle in the World

The Triumph pioneered vertical twin cylinder o.h.v. engine, famed for its power output, economy and complete reliability.

TRIUMPH ENGINEERING COMPANY LIMITED · MERIDEN WORKS, ALLESLEY · COVENTRY · ENGLAND
TELEGRAMS: "TRUSTY, COVENTRY"   TELEPHONE: COVENTRY 60221/2

The Triumph pre-unit (separate gearbox) vertical twin-cylinder engine was produced in 499cc and 649cc engine sizes and powered many of Britain's most popular models during the 1950s, including the Speed Twin, Tiger 100, Thunderbird, Tiger 110 and finally in 1959, the twin-carburettor Bonneville.

Besides the need for larger engine sizes and more speed as larger capacity machines, the period also saw a number of newly conceived 250cc British designs. And it was the Redditch-based Royal Enfield concern which had the distinction of being the first, when it announced its new 248cc Crusader OHV single-cylinder model in August 1956. It was also the first unit construction design of the capacity to be launched by a major British manufacturer in the post-war era. And so Enfield stole a march on its rivals and in doing so created a model range that was to run for a decade.

The late 1950s saw the introduction of several brand new 250cc-engined British designs. The first of these, the Royal Enfield Crusader with its OHV construction power unit debuted first in August 1956. This machine has the optional Airflow fairing.

The year 1958 saw the arrival of a whole crop of new 250s. The first of these, the AJS Model 14, and its twin brother, the Matchless G2, were launched at the Swiss Show in Geneva during March 1958, the result of parent company AMC's decision to return to the popular 250cc class for the first time since the Second World War.

Although at first glance the new AMC power unit appeared radically different from what had gone before at the Plumstead works in South London, in practice the new engine followed familiar ground with a built-up crank-shaft and many of the traditional AMC features. Although the engine appeared to be of the unit construction type, there was in fact a separate gearbox.

In an era when wheel size was almost always 19in or 18in, the 17in wheel used on the AMC two-fifties was notable. But what let the Model 14 and G2 down was the weak brakes and front forks, which had come from the Francis-Barnett/James parts bin.

A larger 348cc version was the AJS Model 8/Matchless G5, appearing in late 1959. There were several differences between the 250 and the new 350, notably the more robust teledraulic forks from the larger 'heavyweight' singles and engine changes.

Next in mid-July 1958 came the futuristic Ariel Leader. Displacing 247cc and with square bore and stroke dimensions of 54 x 54 mm the Leader was Ariel's first two-stroke since 1914, but this was only one of many unusual features of the machine. The styling was controversial to say the least, as was the full enclosure of the engine-gearbox assembly and comprehensive, in-built weather protection. In fact, Ariel claimed in its official press release: 'In all but extremes of bad weather the Leader can be ridden without the need for special clothing. Steel pressings are employed for the frame and bodywork and the side panels are readily removable to provide access to the power unit.' Quite simply, the designer Val Page and his team had set out to provide owners with a very usable deluxe small-capacity touring bike.

To understand *why* the Leader emerged as it did one has to study the motorcycling world as it was in the mid-to late 1950s. Unlike today, the requirements then were entirely different: motorcycles were not seen as purely leisure-time toys for the well-off; instead

The sensational Ariel Leader. Not only did it have a twin-cylinder two-stroke engine, but several innovative features including beam, pressed-steel chassis, comprehensive enclosure and weather protection, and a wide range of additional equipment. For its day it was truly revolutionary. A naked, cheaper version, the Arrow, was put on sale later.

A Leader, two up
in London traffic
during the late
1950s at Hyde
Park Corner.

Another important
British 250cc
design was the
BSA C15 Star,
which arrived in
September 1958.
This featured
a 249cc
(67 x 70mm)
single-cylinder
four-stroke engine,
in unit with a four-
speed gearbox.
It was to spur
a family of BSAs
in this guise with
engine capacities
of 343cc, 441cc
and finally 500cc.

they combined transport to work during the week with touring to the country on high days and holidays.

Later the Leader was also sold in naked form as the Arrow and later still the Arrow Sport (more commonly known as the Golden Arrow). As sold the original Leader came with white-walled tyres, copying the fashion found on certain cars, notably American models, at that time.

In September 1958 BSA introduced the C15. This unit construction 249cc OHV single replaced the long-in-the-tooth C12, itself closely related to the even older C10. In comparison with the machine it replaced, the C15 Star was a much more modern design. At its launch, however, it was very much a softly tuned, good all-rounder for the rider who wanted a ride-to-work machine with reliability, dependability and comfort, rather than outright performance.

250 OHV STAR MODEL C.15

This is the already famous B.S.A. 250 Star with many fine features.

The engine design of the C15 Star was very similar to that of the 199cc Triumph Tiger Cub, except that the cylinder was vertical, rather than being inclined forwards as with the Triumph.

Launched at the end of 1958 to celebrate the diamond jubilee of the Norton company, the aptly named Jubilee was something of a rarity in British bike circles of the 1950s, as it was not only a twin, but with unit construction and ultra-short stroke bore and stroke dimensions (60 x 44 mm), displacing 249cc. Like the two AMC models, the Jubilee utilised the forks and brakes from the Francis-Barnett/James two-strokes. Even so, as it was a four-stroke, Norton were able to ask a premium price compared to rivals who could only offer singles or two-stroke twins.

The appearance of the Jubilee was nothing if not distinctive. There was a

The BSA C15 was manufactured in a wide range of guises: tourer, sports, scrambling trials, police and military types. This photograph shows the Australian police motorcycle training school in Canberra, putting riders through an ultra-tough training schedule, with their BSA two-fifties.

This rider of a 499cc Velocette Venom consults his map whilst touring Scotland during the summer of 1959.

stylish rear fairing consisting of two
quickly detachable side panels (each
held on by a trio of Dzus fasteners)
and a rear portion embracing the
number plate and lamp. At the front
there was a deeply valanced, flowing
mudguard with a guttered edge.

Finally the factory constructed a
specially prepared gold-plated Jubilee
machine to highlight the company's
sixty years in production.

In addition to the models
described earlier in this chapter there
were two of Velocette's most famous

and well-loved models, in the shape of the Viper three-fifty and Venom
five-hundred. The first details of these two high-performance OHV singles
came in the autumn of 1955.

In many ways these two bikes were the closest any manufacturer got to
BSA's famous Gold Star. In fact with its range of tourer, scrambler, enduro
and sportster, the Velocette singles tracked the Gold Star almost one-
for-one.

Based on the MAC (350) and MSS (500) the Viper and Venom benefited
from not only improved performance but also more powerful brakes.

Even companies
such as Velocette
jumped on the
enclosure
bandwagon. This is
the 1959 panelling
as fitted to the
Viper/Venom
sports models.
But it proved
unpopular and was
soon discarded.

Velocette was
much more
successful with
its Clubmans
version of the
Viper/Venom.
Specification
included higher
compression ratio,
modified valve
gear, racing-type
magneto, Amal TT
carburettor, lower
handlebars and rev
counter. The 350
Viper Clubman
could top 100mph;
the 500 Venom
Clubman 110mph.

The late 1950s saw the beginning of foreign imports from a number of Continental European countries, notably Germany and Italy. However, because of tariffs on non-Commonwealth goods, machines such as this NSU 247cc Supermax with overhead cam single-cylinder engine were considerably more expensive than British machines, and therefore sold in relatively few numbers.

The Viper was capable of 91 mph and the Venom 102 mph. Later, Clubmans racing versions of both were made available, and offered even more 'go'.

During the late 1950s (and into the early 1960s), enclosure – concealing parts of a motorcycle behind decorative bodywork, as opposed to adding streamlining to improve performance – gained favour with several British manufacturers. The most notable of these was without doubt the Ariel Leader, which provided virtually complete rider protection and also pioneered the use of plastic components on motorcycles.

Triumph and Norton offered rear enclosure on several of their twin-cylinder models; the Triumph 'bathtub' rear enclosure debuting on the 350cc 3TA Twenty-One during 1957. It was later adopted on several other models, including the 5TA Speed Twin, Thunderbird and Tiger 110. Norton models included the Jubilee, 88 and 90 deluxe versions. Velocette used enclosure for the bottom half of its 350 and 500cc singles for a limited period, whilst Royal Enfield favoured a comprehensive fairing and screen for its Airflow models as a standard fitment, but without any form of rear enclosure.

Subsequently, enclosure went out of fashion, but then made a triumphant return in the mid-1990s with machines such as the Ducati Paso and Honda CBR 600/1000 models. But the British motorcycle industry had shown the way, as it had done in several other areas over the years, including four-valves-per-cylinder and foot-change positive-stop gearboxes.

FURTHER READING

Bacon, Roy. *British Motorcycles of 1940s and 1950s.* Osprey, 1989.

Bacon, Roy. *The British Motorcycle Directory.* The Crowood Press, 2004.

Davies, Ivor. *It's a Triumph.* Haynes, 1980.

Poynting, Roy. *The Sammy Miller Museum Collection: Racing & Sporting Machines.* Redline Books, 2009.

Tratatsch, Erwin. *The New Illustrated Encyclopaedia of Motorcycles.* Grange Books, 1993.

Walker, Mick. *Ariel: The Complete Story.* The Crowood Press, 2003.

Walker, Mick. *The BSA Gold Star.* Redline Books, 2004.

Walker, Mick. *Douglas: The Complete Story.* The Crowood Press, 2010.

Walker, Mick. *Matchless: The Complete Story.* The Crowood Press, 2004.

Walker, Mick. *Velocette Production Motorcycles.* The Crowood Press, 2006.

Walker, Mick. *Motorcycle Evolution, Design, Passion.* Mitchell Beazley, 2006.

Walker, Mick and Carrick, Rob. *Villiers: Everybody's Engine.* Redline Books, 2010.

Wilson, Steve. *British Motorcycles Since 1950* (six-volume series). Patrick Stephens, 1982–1992.

Wright, David. *Vincent: The Complete Story.* The Crowood Press, 2005.

PLACES TO VISIT

Coventry Transport Museum, Millennium Square, Hales Street, Coventry CV1 1JD. Website: www.transport-museum.com A superb display of Coventry-built motorcycles.

Glasgow Transport Museum, 1 Bunhouse Road, Glasgow G3 8DP. Website: www.glasgowmuseums.com. A wide range of British motorcycles, many in un-restored condition.

National Motorcycle Museum, Coventry Road, Bickenhill, Solihull, West Midlands B92 0EJ. Website: www.nationalmotorcyclemuseum.co.uk The largest collection of British motorcycles in the world.

National Motor Museum, Beaulieu Abbey, Hampshire SO42 7ZN. Website: www.beaulieu.co.uk. Now one of the oldest surviving motor museums, but has also always had a range of motorcycles.

Sammy Miller Museum, Bashley Cross Roads, New Milton, Hampshire BH25 5SZ. Website: www.sammymiller.co.uk. Magnificent display of road and competition motorcycles, many of which are very rare.

INDEX